BEGINNING A MAGICKAL LIFE AND PRACTICE

Kingdom Magick (Vol. 2)

BY *Elijah Autumn*

Introduction

Thank for your purchase of Kingdom Magick volume two. This book is the second in the Kingdom Magick series.

In Kingdom Magick volume one, I discussed the basic idea of Kingdom Magick, and to a few points of evidence that I believe help to prove that magick itself is neither good, nor evil. It explained the basic concept that both miracles and magick, all originate from within us, and are both one in the same.

The basic idea behind Kingdom Magick was to help teach those within the Christian faith, which may feel led to magickal principals, that what they are feeling, isn't as evil as their peers often try to teach. Rather, it is a higher calling, and an awakening to a higher consciousness.

What separates good magick and bad, is the manifested intentions of the practitioners, rather than the magickal power itself. The power, simply is what it is. It is truth regardless of misinterpretation. It is, as it was, since creation began.

Kingdom Magick as discussed in volume one is the power that resides in all of us since birth. Jesus called it the kingdom of God (Kingdom of spirit). It is where the spirit resides, and is the source of all miracles and magick that has been documented throughout history. God is a spirit and all that makes up God resides in each of us. We simply need to be opened to it.

If you have not read volume one, I urge you to. Kingdom Magick stems from principals found in many faiths and is eclectic in its fashion. It takes principals found in faiths such as original Christianity, Wicca and others. It applies them together in a way that confirms an undeniable underlined truth.

Kingdom Magick isn't a religion, it's a practice. It is a practice of seeking and learning. It is sharing and experiencing with others like minded in magick and spirituality.

It is having an open mindset and being open to an overall truth that is not limited by corporate religions and dogma.

All quotes and phrases between the chapters are from the author Elijah Autumn.

ISBN 13 # 978-0615974095

ISBN 19# 0615974090

Table of Contents

"I saw a light that pointed my way out of the darkness of my despair. It was within my own heart. Yet, it had been covered by the veil of my surroundings, and I had been blinded to the truth of my own self."

Finding the magick within

The power that was seen in Jesus and the prophets, and the power that is seen in each and every real practitioner of magick today, has learned of such power due to an awakened soul. It was through an intervention of spirit that each of us here, has gained the real knowledge of what dwells within us.

I wasn't one that ever thought much of the idea of reincarnation, or its principals, till one day the spirit enlightened to me to the fact, that much of what I was learning, I simply already knew. Ever had that feeling? If you're like me I know you have. It raised questions within me at that point.

I noticed as a child that I would strangely know and understand things, which others seemed to have to study vigorously, and seemed to struggle to discover. I noticed, that when I read books concerning the subjects of magick, I would find myself already possessing a knowledge of the material, as if I had read the book previously or had already mastered its concept. I remember that it threw me for a loop on how that was even possible?

The reasoning I believe, might be pretty simple. I believe our individual spirits hold all the compiled memories of all our past lives. If we can tap into that knowledge in our present state, then we have a massive amount of data and knowledge to move on, don't we?

Through spiritual intervention our souls can be awakened to the knowledge of our spirit. We must understand that a soul is created by both spirit and physical body combined together.

This intervention of spirit can come in many forms and fashions. It can be from our own seeking of the Divine, or it may come from other enlightened individuals, asking for such intervention on our behalf.

It comes from a true desire to seek truth. It is often found outside the box of the normal corporate religions, and is matter of the Divine experience.

It begins much like an epiphany and ends as a spiritual revelation. Through open minded study and an openness to the Divine, a confirmation of truth is revealed to us, and with it, the real faith to act on our new understanding. At that moment, a new wisdom has birthed within us. It is however, a truth that always was, and that will be forever to come.

Within our physical bodies lie our spirit. When we can begin to merge that spirit, with our mind and our body, and do so in a way where they can work in conjunction together, we begin to understand and see things in a whole new light.

It is my belief, and I believe others would confirm this as well. Many of us as witches or practitioners of magick and miracles, were born what we are, not simply learned. Yes, we must discover and find our true self. We must learn to follow the path that cries out within us, and not to passively follow that which others would wish for us instead. Yes, we must learn and grow and study from infancy, as any student would, but I believe there are several of us here on this earth that hold the destiny as the healers and lovers of this Earth and of real truth.

We carry this wisdom and knowledge from life to life, and with each life we grow in wisdom and understanding. Some of us might move faster than others, but each moves as the Divine calls them, in their own time.

If the essence of magick draws you, then perhaps there is a good chance that this calling of being a healer of love and light resides in you as well? Perhaps it what you once were, and it now calls you again?

When each of us move towards that call it is our experiences, traditions and moral values that we put into it and it is that combination that creates either a good or bad manifested magick from our intentions.

We must understand this important note. In searching for truth, and to our true inner self, there are along with our own spirit, many other spirits. These spirits are all around us. With each good and evil practitioner, comes another spirit. There are also spirits throughout the spiritual plane not in the physical. Remember that not every spirit will guild you to truth and fulfillment, but many will simply attempt to deceive for both monetary (money), physical or spiritual gain. Test each spirit and research every claim.

Remember to trust your intuition. Focus on the inner voice that silently speaks in the recesses of your mind and learn to act on it. My worse situations came when I doubted the voice within me. Had I always followed it, I don't believe I would have encountered half the pain in this life that I have endured.

Don't misunderstand me, I do realize that it is in the troubles of life that often teaches us some of the greatest of all lessons, but how many of us have perhaps encountered the same pain over and over again, simply because we have failed to listen to that voice of wisdom and understanding within us?

Learn to grow from your lessons and appreciate them. Never become stagnant, but always remain searching for fresh flowing rivers of knowledge and wisdom. Submerge yourself in them, and let the spirit of fear *never* hold you back, but trust in love and in truth, and your way will become clear.

Here is an newspaper article I wrote February of 2013. It speaks on destiny and the two factors that I believe make up for a successful journey.

...Destiny is a word that is packed full of challenges. It requires a series of choices and decisions that point our way down each and every path. These choices and decisions are what will

eventually lead us to our final walk, and to each of our destinies. These two actions however depend on two factors.

Complete trust and complete freedom are the determining factors that will decide whether our destinies will be fulfilled or whether they will not. Destiny is indeed the outcome designed for each of us, but I'm here to tell you fear and spiritual confinement can put a brick wall around you and can stop all good things from coming your way.

Free will is a gift of the Divine. It allows for our victories and our failures. In each, whether it be victory or failure a choice was made and a path was chosen. On our journey we will be on many paths, regardless of what any man may claim.

There are many paths leading to the same direction, though they may appear as they do not. These paths will cross each other at different points and times, and though each of us may be walking down a different pathway presently, understand this, that in no way means we won't end up at the same final location at the end.

Each time a failure comes from our choice or decision a lesson is learned and a new path becomes clear. Do not judge anyone for their present path but understand that if they are led by the spirit it is for a valid reason.

Our salvation and destiny does not come from man's law or church membership but solely and completely through spiritual intervention. Yes, we do learn things from our teachers, our mentors and our spiritual leaders but salvation comes from an epiphany that leads to revelation. To have that, we must have trust and complete freedom.

Along with our destiny each of us searches for true love. But true love requires a freedom that has no bounds, for real love has no conditions of merit or standard. It requires a trust that supersedes natural human limits but is metaphorically simply set free within us as kaleidoscope of brilliant emotions that carry us to a world that only lovers can imagine.

It is a free flow of perfect love and perfect trust. These two actions are carried on our choices and our decisions on how we will approach life and people. Yes, there are pains that come with trust, but in it, we believe that in the pain we were taught a lesson and have become stronger people from it.

What is all this saying? It's simple really. Throughout the world we find people scrambling and searching for love, their purpose, their calling, and to simply find something to truly believe in, when the whole time, all that they had searched for, already lied within them. Even Jesus said that the Kingdom of God is within us. It isn't any outward kingdom where we find salvation and contentment, it is within us.

The issues lies in our choice, of do we trust and do we decide on freedom? Does our life allow for free choice and free love? Are we full of judgment or are we full of grace? Do we love with conditions, or do we love unconditionally? Are we free to walk our path without condemnation, and condemnation can come from us as well as others? Can we trust the spirit enough to walk into darkness and to love when pain may certainly be an outcome?

Freedom comes from trust doesn't it? Trust in something bigger than we are. Its trust in the Divine, and knowing that if our intentions are true, the spirit will not fail us no matter how dark things may appear at the present time. We know and understand that in all things good and bad, good can come from it.

We are not slaves to the world but are free to the spirit and understand life and creation for all that it is. We refuse to be bound by vain law but chose to fly with the eagles and to feel even though not every emotion is a pleasant one. We are free, are you ?

"Be free of the religious constraints created by mankind. Love without limits. Run free without fear, and let the inner you shine brighter than all the stars beheld by the vision of others. Be you, and not what others wish you were."

Rules of engagement

With any form of magick there has to be rules. Using magick without rules leads to only one thing and that is real turmoil and despair. Yes, your prayers and spells will indeed go out and will more than likely have their intended effect, but if not within the boundaries of the rules of engagement, they will may very well also come with an avalanche of serious and devastating consequences.

The first thing we must remember, is that whatever we send out in magick, will in time return to us. If we strike out in anger or wrath, then that very same anger or wrath can return to us in a way that is very unwanted and very undesirable.

If we send out love and healing than that same love and healing will return to us as well. I believe we all would say to have that come, would be a much better a situation and favorable outcome to each of us then say the other.

The key to preventing harmful or painful consequences is to understand the reasoning behind the rules and to the learning of self-discipline and emotional management. Without these things you can never achieve a good balance and harmony with life and of creation.

How we feel in any given situation can indeed effect our manifestation of magick. It can indeed amplify our intentions, but it can also adversely affect the outcome or desire of our spells by projecting our inward silent emotions. Meaning simply that though our spoken words may declare one thing, our real emotional intentions always find their way through, and another unpleasant outcome may frighteningly surface at a later time.

Kingdom Magick is about balance. It is gray in all sense of the word. The true practitioner that wants and seeks after real truth will understand and realize that in life and creation there is both a light and dark side of things. Their colors often represent the nature of things that surround us.

In nature there is both life and death. There is fear and then there is love. There is the sun and there is the moon. There is good and then there is evil. In all creation there is a balance.

Through an understanding of this, we can grasp the concept that it is not the nature of things that can be labeled as good or bad, because it simply is, what it is.

Evil manifestations are created by fear or a lack of understanding and wisdom. It is not the magick that is evil but it is the misunderstood or the dark intentions of the evil practitioner.

This Means that the practitioner has chosen to focus on the dark side of nature rather than light. Looking on aspects such as death rather than life. Perhaps they focus on control rather than freedom? Maybe pain over pleasure? The basic meaning is simple however, they manifest dark intentions.

The rules of engagement when it comes to magick center on much of this balance and it is imperative for us to understand that there is a cause an effect on everything we do in the magical arena.

If I were to list just a few off the top ten things _not_ to do in practicing magick, I believe I would offer this bit advice to any and all that sought it.

Here are just a few.

> **1.)** *Never cast any spell against the free will of another human being.*
>
> **2.)** *Attempt in all manner not to alter the natural order of life and creation.*

3.) *Attempt with all measure to do no harm to others, but rather with purest love, practice healing and a mindset of grace.*

4.) *Understand the differences in all people and seek earnestly to live in peace with all of them rather than to make war.*

5.) *When using magick to protect ourselves or another individual, seek an approach that is mainly defensive rather than offensive.*

With this said, what we must remember is that though we

need these rules to help us from crossing the lines that should never be crossed, in the heart of all of it, comes a willingness to simply submit to the guidance of our inner voice and to that of the spirit.

No simple set of rules can take the place of a true spiritual connection with the Divine and to have in that connection a bond that becomes the grandest teacher and guild that any man or woman can desire.

Complete and unwavering truth comes from spiritual revelation and no amount of books or literature can offer more.

The greatest wisdom lies in the understanding of life and of the balance that keeps it. Each of us on this magickal journey must come to grasp with this concept.

"Let not the walls of intolerance worry you. Let not the bias hatred towards your practice, cause you fear. For you shall rise greater than any before and shall shake the foundation of the earth with your roar!"

Love Magick

Magick, as discussed in volume one of Kingdom Magick is simply the manifested intention of the practitioner. Although we do use tools to aid in our focus and to amplify our intentions please remember that true magick is in the practitioner, not the tools.

Let's begin with my favorite, love magick. Love is in my opinion the strongest of all emotions. It can harness an abundance of spiritual and manifested power to anyone understanding its true concept.

Love comes in many forms, but sadly not all everyone in their present life will experience them all.

Some will only experience a few and a few shall never seem to experience any. Regardless however, love is real and it is very powerful.

I have upon this path, come to understand love in a way that I believe can only be gained through spiritual insight and real experience. The differences that can make up the true definition of love are a key to the door of understanding and to the balance of such emotion.

The love for a friend or a spouse is quite different then say a brother or sister. The love a person would have for any enemy is yet another form of the same emotion. It is one word holding many meanings. Is it conditional love or is it unconditional?

Here is an article I wrote for a local newspaper in their spirituality page in January of 2013.

... *Unconditionally, what meaning does that word hold for you? If we apply that word to love, is it something that can touch your heart? To love unconditionally,*

*without boundaries or limitations,
is something every human on earth
I believe has endeavored to find.*

*Unconditional love has no
conditions of merit or standard but
merely is and forever real and
holding. It burns within the
kingdom of God that resides within
us and sees no mistakes but sees
only grace and unending love. It
wraps around us as angels wings
and holds us in the storms of
raging chaos no matter what we
have done or what circumstance we
are walking in.*

*Unconditional love has no
judgments or condemnation, but
knows only that love is the key to
the doorway of all our destinies.
Many will say that unconditional
love is simply a word that cannot
hold true, but I beg to differ.*

Unconditional love can indeed only come when we lay down our words of criticism or accusations, but it is real. You may see someone that in your eyes may walk in sin, yet understand this before you jump to conclusion. In each of our spiritual walks, the spirit walks us down many paths in order to teach us our course of study. Don't criticize or accuse any soul, for they may be exactly where they are intended to be and your words of good intention may hinder the very plan of God.

Unconditional love must offer choice and free will. In offering this, it is inevitable that mistakes will be made and expected. The spirit knows we will probably fail as many times or more than we have victory, but this is the course of our salvation we walk. How dare any soul condemn another while not yet attaining perfection themselves?

We all must learn, and to learn we must experience. Even in the darkest of our times, when emptiness and loneliness fill us with a sense of hopelessness, it is then that we learn and experience emotions and spirituality that will mold us into an awakened soul.

For a faith where its Savior taught not to judge, it seems the church or at least the people within it, have fingers ready to point and words that are ready to ready to cut. There is a difference between using truth to sharpen a friend's sword than it is to cut down a man simply because he has yet to attain the same robe of righteousness that you currently wear. Judge not for the man or woman you now judge may soon wear the very crown on your head instead of you.

Unconditional love whether it be for woman or a man or a brother or sister. Apply these words with gentle direction in love and watch the storms of their lives begin to settle. Offer a hand of love and gentleness and simply leave the rest to the spirit.

Do you not know that we entertain angels unaware? There is a work going on around us all and we need each other for the things that are to come will break even the strongest of hearts.

Trust in the Divine and understand that love was not meant to have restrictions or limits, but true love is boundless and is available to all that understand it.

Never give up, for we are all merely learning to love. Love each other and you shall rise up a people of the spirit of God.

When practicing magick, and when wishing to cast spells of love and say spells such as desire and passion, we must fully understand that to alter any individuals free will of choice, is a disaster waiting to happen.

Love spells must be done in a manner not infringing on such free will. If not the magick we practice is somewhat dark and can very well return to us just as dark in time.

So, how can we as practitioners of magick utilize our gifts of knowledge and use our ability to manifest our intention, and yet still be in line with proper balance?

I like to use love magick in a manner much like fishing. We don't normally seek after one particular fish within the waters do we? Rather, what we do is we bait the hook and wait for a fish desiring it, to bite what we have dressed our hook with, correct?

Well, let's approach our love magick much in the same manner. Let's dress ourselves with the needed bait to catch the fish of our intentions. Let's prepare ourselves for a journey of expectations and a bounty of interested individuals. All without infringing on their free will.

What is it we seek? This is the first thing we need to examine within ourselves. Being very careful to understand our true intentions. Our real intentions, somehow hidden within our spells, indeed have a real way of slipping through, no matter the words spoken.

We must have clear intentions, for it is most often the intention that is manifested, not simply the physical words spoken.

We must ask ourselves, do we seek a lasting love, or simply

someone to share an experience with? Do we long for a soul connection, or do we simply seek the physical?
Understanding these inward desires is the key to achieving our goals and to manifest our utmost power.

Let's start with this, do you personally consider yourself as either sexy or say beautiful? If not, then this is our first spell we need to cast. How we feel about ourselves personally can and will have dramatic effects on the ability of love spells to manifest themselves.

I'm sure all of us have at one time or another heard that beauty is in the eye of the beholder. I'm here to tell you, that this statement couldn't be any truer. People see the manifested gifts within us as we walk, even though we may not particularly see them. The light of these gifts shine within us, and grab the attention of all those that either desire after them, or that possess gifts much of the same.

Let's ask ourselves, are we aware of these gifts? Do we really understand ourselves, or do we need to self-examine for a moment?

Perhaps we do understand some of our own attributes, yet desire something more in our lives? Could this be something you are considering? It is perfectly acceptable to desire more in our lives then what we see. Never let anyone tell you otherwise. We just shouldn't consider ourselves any lesser than anyone else, simply because we have a different gift, or attribute than say another person.

Once we know and understand what it is about ourselves we wish to either to blossom, or create, then we can begin preparing for our spell.

Let's say for a moment we want to manifest the magickal sensuality within us. We wish to show our love for magick in order to draw the interest of another individual having the same magickal sensual desires. We wish to find a lover that appreciates the beauty of nature and of life itself. We wish to find someone that we can relate to within our soul, as it manifest its dreams into physical happiness. No matter our outward appearance, the beauty of who we are inwardly, will always shine as a beacon to anyone searching.

Let's do a basic spell on making this inward sensuality shine outward to the world. (Much like a self-esteem spell)

Soon we will talk about moon phases and particular days of the week that are best to do certain spells, but for now, let's just grasp the concept of learning to visualize our intentions while using a few tools of the craft.

For this spell, we will use these tools. Please note that you may add to or take away from the list as you grow and understand the basic concepts.

We will also be preforming the spell at night.

1. *One orange candle (attraction)*
2. *One pink candle (Love)*
3. *One red candle (passion)*
4. *One sage stick*
5. *ylang ylang oil or patchouli oil* (or any other incense or oil)

Before we begin, I suggest finding a musical selection that tends to calm or to sooth you. This will help focus your intention. Go ahead and start your music if you have it.

Take your lit and now smoldering sage stick and use it to clean away any negative energies in or around your sacred space which is most often an altar. See the chapter for preparing your alter for more. If you choose you may even cast a circle as described in volume one. The sage will however cleanse the area.

Be sure that the candles used are new and unburnt candles.

Never use a previously lit candle for a new spell.

Now let's take our candles and place them in whatever layout you choose within our cleansed space. Light our oils or incense to begin infusing the air with their aroma. Now light the candles.

Remember the magick isn't in the tools, it's in the person.

Within your sacred space sit and begin to focus on what your intentions are. Allow the music to calm you. Let the aroma of the incense or oil fill your nostrils.

With our eyes partially open begin to breathe in through the nostrils and back out of the nostrils. Focusing on each breath as you keep within your mind's eye our desired intentions.

Allow yourself a few minutes to escape the outside world and to enter into your magickal space.

Once you feel yourself calm and focused begin speaking the intentions you wish to manifest. In this case it is our sensuality that we wish to bring to a visual surface.

Here is an example. You may use this one, or simply adapt another one of your own. Visualize what you are saying actually taking place. Make your visualization a reality.

Proceed to say the words in this chant three times....3X

"Upon this night, with candles glowing

Within my space, the winds are blowing.

Love and light ... passion and desire ... may they rise from within me ... and draw my admirer.

As a beacon shines its brilliant light, so shall mine... be just as bright ...upon this night."

Repeat this until you can begin to see within your mind's eye your intentions physically manifesting themselves. See each emotion or characteristic rising to the surface and emitting a glow about you.

Another great thing to consider is carrying stones that emit the energy we desire or need. Here are few great stones. Later, I will discuss how to cleanse and charge our particular stones, and how to cleanse the negative energy out from within our space

1. *Rose quartz*
2. *Clear quartz*

3. *Moonstone*
4. *Jade*
5. *Emerald*

With working with love magick, or any magick really, all that is needed to change or vary our spells, is to change our tools and our spoken words, to watch our desires and inward intentions.

Just remember that different candles or better said, their particular colors, work differently. Their individual colors hold different energies and can assist us greatly when such energy flows with our intention.

Here are a few great colors that are great for love magick spells.

We used these earlier, but never bad for a review.

1. *Red candles – For sexual love (passion)*
2. *Pink candles – For love of the heart*
3. *Orange candles – great for attraction.*
4. *White candles- Great for purity, emotional healing and for protection.*

All we must do is understand the rules of engagement in our spells, and adjust as I said, our spoken words and tools to match our intentions.

Whether it be strictly a spell for added passion in a relationship, or an attraction spell for a wandering eye, or to even catch someone's eye, simply follow the basic format and adjust as needed.

"Freedom is more then not being locked with four walls. But it is the openness of free expression, and the true ability to walk without fear, or worry in a world, so mentally and emotionally confined".

Cleansing and charging

In the previous chapter I mentioned about using crystals and stones. I personally love the beauty and power these stones can have in our lives.

Each stone harnesses its own personal energy, and that energy can infuse in our daily lives through carrying them in our packets, or in bags. They can be worn around the neck as a necklace, or cut to fit on a beautiful ring. The hobby of creating these wonderful masterpieces is one of my favorites. I find it amazing to see the intricate designs that true lovers of magick can produce.

But even with the beauty and artistic designs, lie something far greater then what the eye can even see. Crystals and stones have within them power. Each stone comes with an energy that can amplify our intentions, aid us in our weaknesses, and even protect us from negative energies.

We can even charge our personal stones with our own desired intentions, much like a casted spell. When we carry them on our person, such energy is released as we go about our daily walks.

But what stones work best for what circumstance? Can we carry more than one stone to aid in multiple areas? If we carry the wrong stone can it impair us or hinder us? These are important questions we must learn as we seek to use crystals and stones on our magickal journey.

<u>Before we go into cleansing and charging let's look at a few good crystals stones for healing and how they work best.</u>

Crystals and Stones

1. **Clear quartz crystals** – Also known as "rock crystal". It is an energizer and an amplifier. It is probably the most powerful and versatile. The stone amplifies the energy from other stones as well. It amplifies our intentions, our spells, our prayers and more. It promotes clarity of thought and inner healing.

2. **Amethyst stone**- Amethyst is a mind stone. It helps to bring a calmness and clarity to the owner. It lowers anxiety and confusion. It is also use for protection, because it repels more than attracts. It is used to enhance intuition and physic ability. To induce visions and is also a great aid in addiction recovery.

3. Rose Quartz – Rose quartz is a stone of warmth and love. It helps to heal emotional pain, and it helps open our senses up to the beauty that surrounds us. The stone enhances all forms of love and helps create a mind frame of unconditional love as it opens our hearts to forgive and heal.

4. Tigers eye – This stone is an excellent grounding stone. It is great for protection, clear thinking and personal empowerment. It promotes strength and balance. It enhances decision making abilities. It has also been used to stimulate wealth and has the needed grounding to aid one in keeping such wealth. It has been said that it helps those suffering from nervousness, ADHD and more.

5. Aquamarine – This stone is a stone of courage. The stone is used to calm or sooth. Perhaps to relieve a person of fear or a phobia. It combats depression and promotes safe travel on water. It assist the owner in a sense of peace, promotes better communications and a greater sense of self awareness.

6. **Agate** – These stones are power stones. There are a great grounding stone. They possess a fantastic protective and healing energy. It is a good stone for those needing an eye for detail such as accountants and bankers. It is great for suffers of stress and emotional pressure.

7. **Moonstone** – This stone is a stone of emotional balance. It is used for child birth, fertility and reproductive restoration. It helps bring together the heart and mind of the owner and an openness to listen to others. It is believed in some cultures that a wearer of the stone would bring themselves new love and can even stop a quarreling couple.

8. Turquoise – This is a stone of spiritual journey and wisdom. The stones enhances communication skills. It is a stone of self-realization and understanding of our inner self. It promotes us to walk in truth and to walk the walk we talk. It helps to absorb negativity. It works to strength both mind and body.

9. Smokey Quartz – This stone has been said to be a stone of co-operation. It has a way of transforming negative energy and bringing multiple energies together. It has a way of calming and soothing. Helps to eliminate such things as panic attacks and nightmares.

10. Jade -This is a stone of prosperity and wisdom. It is known as a stone of luck and longevity. It enhances discernment and confidence. It has been known to help in remembering dreams and to aid in our realization of our spiritual self.

These ten stones are but a small hand full compared to the many beautiful ones that we will use in our spiritual journey. I urge each reader to go out and get themselves a good book on the characteristics and energies of each crystals and stones. It will be a great tool on your path.

Now that we know a few good stones and how they work, how do we go about cleaning them, and charging them? Is there an exact method, or can each practitioner somewhat create their own methods?

Although we all can alter many of the trades and approaches of how to perform certain things in the craft, I believe many of the things we do should be traditional, and in that, it helps create within ourselves a form of discipline.

Before we do anything we need to cleanse them. By doing this we need to understand that we are cleaning more than the outer appearance of our stones but we are cleaning away all negative energies and unwanted aspects of the stones that may have been absorbed by former owners.

When I cleanse my stones and crystals I like to think of it as a ritual of sorts. Perhaps not in as much depth or detail, but regardless, the process is very important.

Before I begin, I first find, my altar. It is a place where I will set up my candles and my incense and my other tools of the craft. In most of my doings, unless I am with a group, I pick a time where I can be alone so that I can focus and amplify the magickal power.

I first, as I normally do, find a good music selection. *Loreena McKennit* is a wonderful singer that creates a surrounding full of serenity and peace. I also find *Wendy Rule* to be fantastic choice for many of my magickal practices.

After starting my music, I will light my candles and my incense. I tend to use white and pink candles for purification and to create an atmosphere of love and peace. As far as incense simply pick one that creates a sense of serenity.

I then use a sage stick to cleanse the room of any negative energy that might have crept in through life's trials and tribulations.

You may wish to say a few words or even cast a circle, but I don't always find it necessary. As I light my candles and cleanse the room with the sage, I merely visualize all the negative energies leaving and the purity and love of the burning candles entering in. All while the music simultaneously creates an environment of divinity.

Now take your stones and crystals and run them under cool water. Visualize the negativity running off of them and leaving as it sinks down the drain of the sink.

Return to your alter or your cleansing station. Now we will charge our stones and our crystals.

Simply place your clear quartz crystals either in the sunlight or the moonlight to charge them. We will return to them later. The light of both will charge them. Many prefer to do so under a full moon as I do once a month. It is a good idea to consider.

For our other stones, grasp in your dominate hand a few of the stones, or all of them if you can hold them without dropping them. I want you to begin to visualize your intentions. See it in your mind's eye. See those intentions flowing through your body, down your arm and into the stones.

Feel and see the magickal energy of your manifested intention filling each stone in your hand. Try seeing this manifestation as a color, watch it as it flows.

Then slowly place your stones on your alter or your station in a glass bowl, or any bowl of choice. Allow the crystals to soak in the light for a couple hours or in the moonlight overnight if possible

Consider what stones you will carry on you and find a sachet or small fabric bag to hold your stones. You can also simply place them in a pocket, but for me, I'm just a little more attentive to my own, and prefer a small cloth bag. I personally have one I carry on me. It is purple with a gold triquetra.

I recommend cleansing your stones depending upon use. If you carry them on you on daily then I recommend cleansing and recharging them at least once a week.

If your crystals and stones merely sit on your alter or other place once a month would probably suffice. Even that however depends highly on the traffic of your home, and to how much negative energy is allowed into the home. Remember anyone walking through your door is also bringing with them all their positive, and yes negative energies. Consider this when you plan your schedule.

"Set your mind to achieve the inner calling of your spirit. For in doing so, your feet shall be firmly planted on the right path for you, and the perfect balance of mind, body and spirit will light up your way".

Wheel of the year

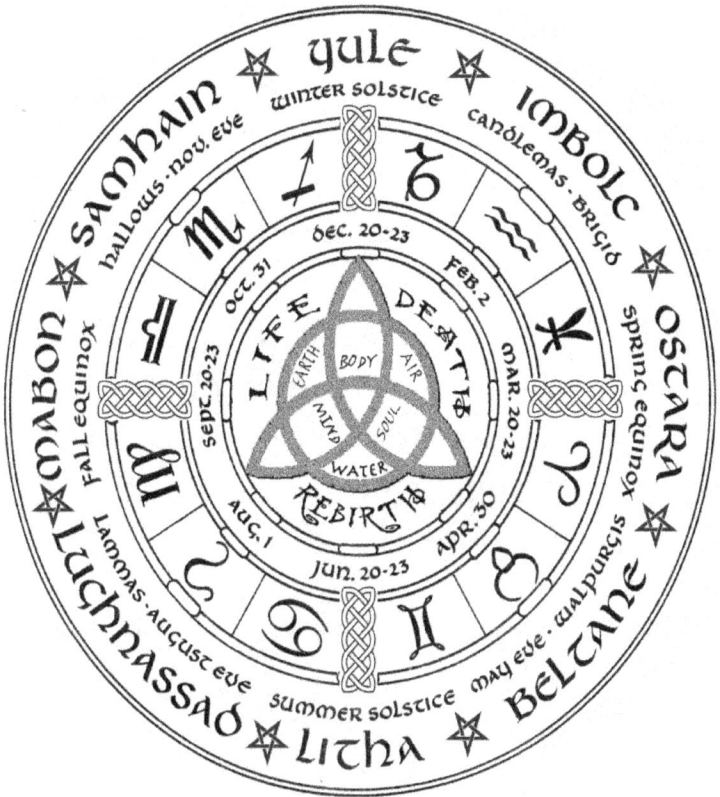

Kingdom Magick follows the wheel of the year. It is an annual cycle of seasonal festivals or Sabbats celebrated by most pagans and others. It consists of eight festivals called the Solstice and the Equinox.

If you look at this chart or the wheel of the year, you will see the eight points of celebrations. These points are extremely important to remember and should be understood and honored.

Here is a list of the eight points. (Quarter days and cross quarter days)

1. (Yule) (Winter Solstice) - (Dec 20-23) recognized as a significant turning point of the year. It is celebrated by everything from sacrifices to Feasting and gift giving. Bringing evergreen and sprigs into homes, and making wreaths and decorating trees.

2. Imbolic (Feb.2) - The first cross quarter day following midwinter and the beginning of what will be spring. It is a time for purification and spring cleaning in anticipation of spring's new life. Too many (Celtics) the festivals is dedicated the goddess Brigid. It is also a tradition time for pledges and re-dedications.

3. **Spring equinox** (Ostara) (March 20- 23rd) – From this day forward days are longer then the nights. It is regarding as a time of rebirth, and is celebrated as a time of great fertility. Eggs are often colored.

4. **Beltane** (April 30th) — Traditionally the first day of summer. It is a time for flowers and dancing. Earliest celebrations were in honor of *Flora*, the roman goddess of flowers. A celebration of light.

5. **Summer Solstice) (Litha)** (June 20-23) — One of the four solar holidays. It is the turning point where summer reaches its height and the days are the longest. It is a time of celebrating the power of the sun. It is a time to celebrate both work and leisure. It is also another fertility sabbat for not only humans but crops and animals.

6. **Lammas (Lughnasadh)**(August 1st) — First of the three Wiccan holidays, The other two being autumn equinox and samhain. Wiccans often celebrate by baking a figure of the god in bread, and eating it to signify the sanctity and importance of the harvest.

Celebrations vary but are most often in thanksgiving for grain and bread.

7. **Fall equinox (Mabon)**(Sept 20-23) -This is a time of Thanksgiving for the fruits of the earth, and time set to recognize the need to share them to secure the need of the goddess and god for the winter to   come.

8. **Samhain** (Oct 31st) – This is considered one of the greatest among the Sabbats. It is a time for celebration of those that have passed on, and to give respects to the dead. It is a festival of darkness, which is opposite the other side of the wheel, called Beltane (Festival of light). It has been a time to invite the spirits of the dead to attend the celebrations. It is in this time that many believe that the veil between this world, and the afterlife is the thinnest and the easiest time to communicate with such spirits.

"Ignorance is the first drop of water that opens to the mighty storm of chaos and despair. With Blind Hatred and bigotry due to tradition or upbringing. Where is the wisdom, where is the understanding?"

The Pentagram

And the elements

The pentagram in medieval Christian tradition was a symbol of the five wounds of Jesus (two wrist, Two feet and his side). In the Renaissance it came to be associated with magick and the occult.

Religions ranging from the Church of the latter day Saints to the Wiccan faith have used, or do use this symbol in their faith or practice.

The Church of the latter day Saint use the symbol as decoration in their temples, and is taken from the Bible scripture of Revelation chapter 12. Where it reads,

"And *there appeared a great wonder in Heaven; a woman clothed with the sun, and the moon under her feet, and upon her head a crown of twelve stars"*.

Though the symbol has been around for centuries. The symbol was seen as early as the 1980's in some Wiccan publications, and was by the 1990's, seen as a traditional symbol of its faith.

The pentagram here is a five pointed star with its one point facing up. The points represent the five elements. A circle around the star unites all the elements with spirit and is called a pentacle. The pentacle is a widely worn amulet, and is seen much on the altars, of magickal people.

It is not to be confused with the inverted pentagram that has an inverted star, sometimes within a circle. This symbol is most often used for evil practices.

Here is an example of a pentagram (without a circle)

used in Kingdom magick, Wicca
and other practices holding
many of the same principles and
values.

In Kingdom Magick we see the
Pentagram just as it is in Wicca.
It is the union of the five
elements.

Spirit

Air

Water

Earth

Fire

At the top of the pentagram we see its point. This point represents spirit. If we are looking at the pentacle on the page, the point directly to the left is seen as the element of air.

If we look to the pentacle at its lower left hand side, we see the element of Earth. If we continue around at the lower right hand side, we see the element of fire. As we reach the top right, we of course see the element of water.

The elements are considered to be the building blocks of the universe. The elements have been compared as such.

1. Air = Thought
2. Fire = Desire
3. Water = Emotions
4. Earth = Stability

➢ **Air** = Air is the element of the East and is connected to the soul .It is also the breath of life. If you're doing a work that is related to communication, wisdom or the powers of the mind, Air is the element to focus on. Air carries away your troubles, blows away strife, and carries positive thoughts to those who are far away. Air is associated with the colors yellow and white.

➤ **Fire** - Fire is a purifying, masculine energy, associated with the South. It is connected to strong will and energy. Fire, both creates and destroys, and symbolizes the fertility of the God. Fire can heal or harm, and can bring about new life or destroy the old and worn. As for color representation, fire is red or orange

➤ **Water** - Water is a feminine energy and highly connected with the aspects of the Goddess. It is used for healing, cleansing, and purification,

Water is related to the West, and associated with passion and emotion. In many spiritual paths, including Catholicism, consecrated Water is used as holy water. It is merely just regular water with salt added to it, and usually a blessing or invocation is said above it. In Wiccan covens, such water is used to consecrate the circle and all the tools within it. As you may expect, water is associated with the color blue.

➢ **Earth** - Earth is connected to the North, Earth is considered the ultimate feminine element. The Earth is fertile and is stable, it is associated with the Goddess. The planet itself is a giant ball of life, and as the Wheel of the Year turns, we all can watch all the aspects of life take place in the Earth: birth,

life, death, and finally rebirth.
The Earth is nurturing and
stable, solid and firm, full of
endurance and strength. In
color, it is represented as both
green and brown connect to the
Earth.

The four elements of earth, air, fire and water are also associated with our astrological signs.

1. **Earth** = *Taurus, Virgo and Capricorn.*
2. **Air** = *Libra, Gemini and Aquarius*
3. **Water** = *Cancer, Scorpio and Pisces*
4. **Fire** – *Aries, Leo and Sagittarius*

Preparing your Altar.

Preparing an altar is different for every practitioner. Some use different objects then others, and this, in most cases is perfectly acceptable.

In most cases an alter will include such things such as candles, bowls, chalice, stones, incense, a pentacle and an Athame (double edge dagger)

In Wiccan and other practices, there will even be one side for the goddess and another for the god.

Your altar is your sacred place. It is the place where you will do most of your spell work, incantations and prayers. All the tools of your particular craft will in most cases be close at hand next to your altar.

Many like to include, on their altar, the elements of earth, air, fire and water. This is done in many way but can be as simple as this.

1. **Water** – A small bowl of water
2. **Fire** - a lit incense or candle burning.
3. **Earth** – a small bowl of salt
4. **Air –** Air is all around us. It is in the smoke from our incense or the flicker in the flame. Even our own breath is a symbol of air.

Many people like to include an assortment of different things. They might even include statues of their particular god or goddess, or they might use objects to simply represent them. There really isn't a right way or wrong way, but simply your way. It is your place where you meet with the Divine, and do most of your spiritual manifestations.

Personally I love to use candles and stones in much of my work. I use the pentacle, but I also love the Triquetra which many have seen in the famous T.V. Show " *Charmed* ". Here is a Triquetra.

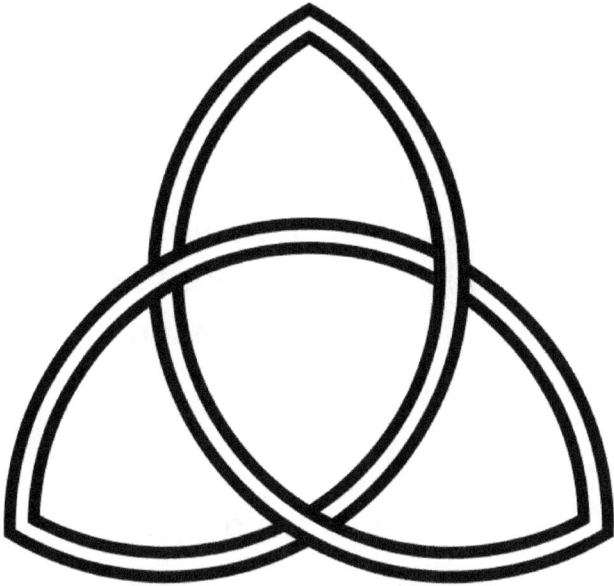

I use either it on or around my altar. You can decorate around your alter with flowers, paintings or anything that helps you focus and relax as you meditate on your intentions. Be you, and set your altar up as you see within yourself.

Try to keep your alter in a place where strangers and common traffic don't hang around it much. Remember that negative energies can linger around, and our alter space needs to be as free of all negative energies as we can get.

The more traffic your sacred space gets, the more you must cleanse it using sage sticks and yes, casting a circle.

It is wise to do so each time you use your alter space if it is heavily trafficked.

Perhaps even keep a journal of all your spell work like you see in the picture. Journals are also called our book of shadows, and include all the spells we have put together and manifested in our alter space.

Perhaps I will do a spot on created a book of shadows in the near future.

The Authors thoughts

As I sit and contemplate various things that fill our world, my spirit is grieved by such an overwhelming tide of negative and harmful influences and practices. I walk each day with a mindset to allow the spirit to inspire, and to teach through various human interactions and experiences. I see religious people proclaiming their truth and I see the sad faces of those lost in despair from not finding it.

Evil indeed fills our world, but my friends, the biggest evil isn't in any religion or practice. It isn't in any particular action or lack of action. The biggest evil on this planet is ignorance, and people hurting each other through a lack of real knowledge and understanding.

Love is a word disappearing from our world. As the people lose more and more understanding of real divinity, the spirit of love slowly is fading into the darkness of man-made theologies and bias hatred towards all of the Divine's children.

Religious people point fingers of judgment as they stand upon a mountain of lost souls that were sadly lost from the making of their own hands. The spirit of the love weeps as real seekers of truth and divinity are cast out because they don't fit into the perfect little boxes created by the modern Pharisees of the modern churches.

There is indeed one truth, but there is not simply one path for us all. The Divine one walks each of us down various paths due to our purpose or call. Each of us learns differently and in a different way. Yes the basic truth is always the same, but the path to that truth may not always be walked by everyone at the same time.

False judgments and harsh statements spoken in what folks call righteous anger can be the sword that doesn't always divide the truth, but more so, often slays the seeking spirit of fragile butterflies that were beautiful in the eyes of God.

Is there a right and a wrong in this world – yes, there is. What we must understand however is that our world isn't just black and white, but most often there is a gray. This gray is where most people live. They don't conjure evil and their knowledge of spirit is minimal at best. They simply walk among the enlightened and are either feed the living water of truth, or they are polluted and beat down by bad people with a little real knowledge. A little knowledge in the wrong hands can be very dangerous in any situation.

Terms and labels have so many stereotyped definitions that people often make judgments and decisions based on preconceived and media pushed teachings. They hear certain phrases or titles and they cast their judgments not based on facts, but on what their tradition has taught them instead.

People point their fingers but refuse to open their hands in acceptance or guidance. The world has traded one book over the direct intervention of spirit. They point out various scriptures intended to cut, yet at the same time they cut out various scripture entirely from the lives themselves and choose to ignore them?

Truth is all around us. The spirit is with us everywhere we go. Don't be afraid to learn from each other. Never set in your mind that you can learn no more, but be a seeker of complete truth. Stop judging those in whom Jesus would have never judged.

Stop playing God and set your mind on simply being what God said your destiny would be. Understand the Kingdom of God is not about talk but about power (1 Cor. 4:20). If you don't see that power then take that first step forward on your path and keep walking into you do.

Can you hear the voice, which echoes off the trees? As the wind blows, it carries with it, the combined voices of all those from the past. It carries with it, the voice of the Divine and all that was, is and is to be. Can you feel in your spirit a pulling that is undeniable? Is there a stirring, beginning to turn within you for real truth, and completed answers? Stop, and listen, for the answers are indeed within your reach. They are answers that have been so simple, yet covered by a mask of human perspective and vain traditions and that have left many so blind.

It isn't that truth is withheld from us, it is that we are have lost the ability to hear and see what lies right in front of our face. We have forgotten where we come from, and to where we all shall go again in the end.

So many people lost in a chaos of religion and schemes. So many people simply wanting the answers to their big questions and still so many dyeing with those questions unanswered- why? Truth is what it is and no measure of human interpretation can alter it.

Truth in itself is not relative but is constant. It is our human perception that creates the relative factors in truth as each person may see things in a different manner depending upon things such as tradition and upbringing. That in no way changes the element of truth that is unchanging however.

We are all students of truth. Each of us can be found on the path of personal salvation and understanding. Any religion that mocks another is a religion not of love but of condemnation. The Holy Bible says in Philippians 2:12 (NIV) *"continue to work out your salvation with fear and trembling,"* Which means simply that it is the sole responsibility of ourselves to find the truth and to our own salvation through the work of the spirit. In 1

Corinthians 16:14 it reads *"Do everything in love."*(NIV)

Love is at the center of real truth. It is in the purpose of creation and why all that we see exists in this world. The Holy Bible says this about love. Reading from 1 John 4:8 (NIV) it declares this. *"Whoever does not love does not know God, because God is love"*

The hard part in many of our lives is that when truth does prick at our heart, we often reject it. We don't want to see it, as it is being shown to us. We decide to accept a version of the truth that might be close, but yet is not what we truly know to be truth at all. It is then that a wall against real knowledge and understanding is built, and our own spiritual growth is severely hindered or even stopped.

The first goal in understanding truth is trust in the Divine and a willingness to walk, even though we may be afraid or even unsure. We must be willing to open our minds and our hearts, and to accept the revelation for what it is.

Fear is at heart of all spiritual failures. Whether it is fear of persecution or fear of the unknown, fear is not of Divine, and should be dealt with. Many people refuse to read anything other than the sixty six books found in the Holy Bible. It is fear that limits them and controls them.

Those that are spirit driven understand that although truth is indeed found in the Bible, it is also found in other books as well, and should be used in the course of all our studies. To refuse the knowledge of those placed here by the Divine, is to refuse the Divine entirely. The Divine speaks even today through all types of people, and in so many types of religions.

We should measure everything we hear and read compared with the confirmation of the spirit.

Take a moment today, and perhaps go the park, or take a stroll on a quiet path. Listen to your surroundings and open yourself to the spirit of truth. The Divine is everywhere at all time and there is no better place to find him then in his creation.